Willful Blindness

There is a term used in law called Willful Blindness and it describes a situation in which a person tries to avoid criminal or civil liability for a wrongful act by intentionally keeping himself or herself unaware of facts that would render him or her liable. People will testify in court that they were around the crime scene but they weren't aware of what was going on. It is a conscious avoidance of the truth. In other words, it's turning a blind eye, trying to ignore or deny the obvious. I wonder how often willful blindness plays out in our everyday lives. Are there blind spots in our families, our marriages, our churches, and organizations? Things that we don't want to see or talk about yet we know are there but we overlook and just go with the flow. Then when chaos erupts, we don't want to be held accountable, or we play the victim! At some point, we must be willing to lift the blinders. Some of us are in dating relationships with red flags popping up that need to be addressed. Some of us have people living in our homes that are doing improper or unlawful things that we need to stop ignoring. If you could have or should have known something but deliberately chose not to, you are still partially liable. Willful ignorance of what's going on at home, work or church is not a defense to keep you from being held responsible. Don't wait until something traumatic happens and then cry "How could I have been so blind?"

-In What Situation Do You Need To Take Off The Blinders?'

Marriage Matters

Marriage is a blessing but we all know that it takes a lot of hard work. Loving a person is one thing… Dealing with a person in all of their glory is another! Here are a few tips that I've learned along the way that I think are essential in keeping a happy, healthy relationship. First off, always remember that your spouse is not your enemy. No matter how upset they've made you, you are on the same team and your goal should be to win together. Honesty and open communication are key to every good relationship. Be honest, even when it's tough. Be kind and forgiving. Your spouse will frustrate you often but love them through it. And don't major on the minors! Not every little thing needs to be addressed. Choose your battles. Say thank you and display appreciation often. Understand that men and women are different. We think differently. Always try to empathize and compromise. You cannot be selfish when you're married. It's no longer just about you. Find other married couples to hang out with. Couples with common interests and values. Have fun. Also, be accepting and encouraging of each other's alone time. I think it's healthy to do things apart from one another every now and then. Lastly, remember that life is full of ups and downs. Your marriage will also experience this. Not every day will be up but not every day will be down. Middle ground is ok (and pretty normal) as long as it's solid. Stay committed and remember the covenant that you made to each other and to God. Marriage is a ministry. Honor it and treat it as such.

-How Is Your Marriage?-

This Thing Called Parenting

I've had conversations recently with a couple of mothers who are experiencing some challenging times with their children, and this has discouraged them and caused them to doubt their parenting skills and choices. I listened and tried to encourage them but I was hesitant to say too much, thinking I am in no way an expert on parenting, but then I remembered that none of us are! So here's my two cents. All I know is that this parenting thing is part joy, and part warfare. None of us do it all 'right', nor do we do it all the same. How do we even define or measure!? There are no instructions or real answers. Every situation is unique. Each child is different with different needs. Each parent has different challenges, as well as different skills, experiences, and abilities so the first thing I urge you to do is not compare yourself or your situations to anyone else. Yes, you will make mistakes but use those mistakes as opportunities. Don't try to be perfect because you won't be! You may have ten kids but each will be different so you will have to parent them all differently. Be willing to change your technique of teaching, and discipline, etc. An imperative key to parenting is learning your child's love language. What do they respond to positively? What motivates them? Be in tune with that. All children will challenge you at some point but love them through it. And please love YOURSELF through it! Don't feel bad because your child doesn't like you at the moment. They'll get over it. As children age, mothers often have a hard time with this, and with letting go. We want to keep them safe and happy, and unburdened by the cares of the world so we offer to let them live with us while they are young adults but please still teach them responsibility. It's ok to make them pay rent, or utility bills. It's ok to tell them when they're wrong! It's ok to make them responsible for cooking and cleaning of their own things. Don't do them a disservice by being an enabler. (Trust me, I speak on this from experience). As parents, we must find the balance between nurturing and protecting while still allowing our children to grow, experiment, and become independent. Parenting is probably the hardest job on earth. It's indeed a daily learning experience. In the end, if you have created a caring, responsible human being then I think you've been pretty successful at this parenting thing. Be encouraged! Lastly, don't forget to keep your children covered in prayer. And remember, they watch more than they listen. You are their example. Right now, you are the face of God.

-How Is Your Relationship With Your Children?-

Living and Loving the Word

I tried to write this book without referencing much scripture. I was striving for the "Inspirational" category more than the "Christian" category. Well, when it's in you, it's in you. I love the Word of God and I can't get around it so I'm sorry (not sorry) if it's too much for you. With that being said, I must warn you that this section is a strong word, laced with scripture, geared toward the men and women of God who are preaching and pastoring our churches because I feel led to speak on it. You see, I grew up going to church every Sunday but I can honestly say that it wasn't until I was an adult and joined Shekinah Glory Bible Fellowship Church in Cedar Rapids, Iowa under Pastor James Toney that my spiritual growth began. Pastor Toney taught the word of God in season and out of season. Sunday morning church service was more like bible study, and Wednesday night bible study was like spiritual boot camp! He always taught the word! And the more I learned the word, the more my faith grew, and my relationship with Christ developed. It's very disheartening for me now thinking about the preachers that aren't teaching the scriptures to their people. The bible says *'My people are destroyed for lack of knowledge.'* (Hosea 4:6) The Apostle Paul told Timothy to *'Study to show yourself approved; rightly dividing the word of truth.'* (see 2 Tim 2:15) Pastors, please stop with the "fluff", the feel-good sermons with no substance or scripture base. Your flock should not sit under you for years and not be able to recite the Roman's Road to validate their salvation. Their foundation should be solid. They should know how to study, and they should be able to disciple others. Hearts are penetrated and convicted by the word of God. Transformation and deliverance comes only through the word! Woe be unto you Pastor if you aren't studying and doing your best to teach the scriptures in order to truly reform lives. The blood will be on your hands (See Ezek 3:17-18). 2 Tim 4 says *'The time will come when they will not endure sound doctrine...*

Make full proof of your ministry.' People are sitting in churches broken and discouraged, wondering why their prayers aren't being answered. Teach the word and tell them to stop praying dysfunctional prayers! James 4:3 tells us that we're not receiving what we ask for because we're asking amiss. We're asking for our lustful desires rather than praying the will of God. Psalm 66:18 states *'If I regard iniquity in my heart, the Lord will not hear me.'* Before the blessings, there is obedience that is required. Please handle God's written word with care. There's so much pain in the pews but understanding and application of God's word is life altering. *'When my heart is overwhelmed, lead me to the Rock that is higher than I.'* (PS 61:2) I don't know how people make it through this life without faith in God but it's my faith that has truly sustained me. *'Thy word is a lamp unto my feet and a light unto my path.'* (PS 119:105) I love God and I love His word. It is so rich, and so many beautiful blessings await us if we would just abide by His word. I hope those of you reading this have a good church covering. I want to say thank you to those pastors that are truly teaching, preaching, and spreading the word of God. We can't live the word and love the word without first learning the word.

-Are you under good leadership that's teaching you the word of God? What will you study on your own this week?-

Generational Curses

We cannot choose our relatives, although I'm sure we'd like the option to shuffle the deck at times. If we look at our extended families, most of us can identify things that seem to be reoccurring problems. Well, those reoccurring problems are curses and are designed to kill, steal, and destroy. Is there emotional instability in your family? Hereditary sickness? Divorce? Poverty? Alcoholism? We may not realize it but someone up the family tree has caused a curse to fall upon the family due to their iniquity (sins) (See Ex 20:5). The effects of sin are often passed down from generation to generation. When a father has a sinful lifestyle, his children are likely to practice a similar lifestyle. Generational curses are real but can be broken with exposure, repentance, and deliverance. God promised to curse Israel's sin upon third and fourth generations but then He right away promised in Ex 20:6 to show mercy unto thousands that love Him and keep His commandments. I'm so thankful for God's grace! If you're worried about a possible generational curse, please accept salvation and keep His commandments. Break the chain for yourself, your children, and your children's children. There's freedom on the other side.

-What Generational Sins Do You Recognize In Your Family That You Are Willing To Expose And Seek Deliverance Of?-

Insensitive People

One day a coworker of mine needed to grab one item from the grocery store. Of course there's Handicap parking, there's Expectant Mother's parking, and now they have a couple of parking spots for Starbucks customers (which is located inside the grocery store). She told me that she would never take a handicap spot but decided that day to take the Starbucks since her purchase was going to be quick. Well, when she returned to her car, there was a handwritten note telling her that the parking spot she took was for Starbucks' customers only and not for fat, lazy people! She tried to act as if it didn't bother her but I am an empath so I took on the feelings for her! I was mortified and then I was sad. How can people be so insensitive!? Sure, she shouldn't have parked there but who would be so ugly as to add the brutal name calling!? Probably someone that would never be tough enough to say it to her face! I had to pull myself together because I really wanted to go hunt that person down and give them a piece of my mind with my fists balled up! Thank God He's changed me! I know that only light can drive out darkness so I had to remember the words of First Lady Michelle Obama "When they go low, we go high." The moral of the story is that we never know someone's situation so we should be slow to speak and never judge. What if she had just lost her husband, had three kids at home, ran in to grab some eggs and because she's been so depressed and stressed she didn't even see the new Starbucks parking sign? What if she had been having suicidal thoughts that day and your note pushed her over the edge? Insensitive people are weak-minded, self-centered, and usually insecure and jealous. I pray this is not you. Please be mindful of what you say to others. You can speak the truth to someone without hitting below the belt and being insensitive and insulting. Conduct yourself as a polished adult. Most of us act the way we do because we've learned it from our family environment. Remember that your children are watching you. In the meantime, figure out the root of your anger.

-When Was The Last Time You Acted Insensitively?

What Will You Do Differently Moving Forward?

Uncommon Relationships

Every now and then we find ourselves thrown into relationships that are complicated and frustrating. Maybe it's with an in-law. Maybe it's your spouse's ex. Whatever the scenario is, don't despise it. Always take the high road and try your best to breathe, disarm, and put in the effort to create a smooth relationship. Some people are harder to deal with than others but if this person is going to be a part of your blended circle then it should be of importance to you to work things out. You can't change others and you may think you don't need to change but it's imperative that you continuously grow. You will find that uncommon relationships will challenge you and force you to expand. Don't run from the relationships, and don't underestimate the importance and value of them. I've seen some uncommon friendships that are beautiful and impactful. Facing these challenges will strengthen you and cause you to be a light and example to others of how it's to be done.

-What Uncommon Relationship Are You Willing To Put More Effort Into?-

Big Sin, Little Sin

Some people believe that some sins are greater than others, and will tell you that not all sins are equal. Well, I believe sin is sin. There's no big sin, no little sin. All sin is deserving of God's wrath. I also believe, however, that the consequences of sin can differ depending on various factors. For example, if our sin was willful and caused numerous people to stumble, we might find God's wrath to be more than if we sinned in our thoughts. In this regard, I guess you could say there are levels to sinning. But ultimately, James 2:10 says '*Whoever shall keep the law, yet stumble in one area, he is guilty of all.*' It doesn't matter if you killed someone, stole something, or had lustful thoughts about someone else's spouse, you're guilty of the same sin. God is disappointed in it all. This is why we are to seek forgiveness daily, and turn from our wicked ways. None of us will ever be sinless but our goal should be to sin less. We're all going to mess up from time to time but don't continue in your sin. When you slip, don't slide.

-Do A Bible Study On Sin-

Money Moves

You can't be completely "polished" without having a good grasp on your financial life. The bible says that we are the head, not the tail. Lenders, not borrowers. (see Deu 28:12-13) God does not want us to live in lack but we each have to take financial responsibility. I am not a financial advisor so I will not go into too much but I have a few pointers. First, please believe that credit matters! Protect your credit score by making on-time payments and not allowing your debt to be turned over to a collection agency. Also, don't accept numerous credit cards. I think having one, no more than two is best, and try to keep your credit card usage under 30% at all times. You want your credit score to be above 700. Having cash is great but credit will get you things that your cash won't. Pull your credit report (Credit Karma is free) and know your starting point. Know how much you have in assets, and what your liabilities are. Don't let past financial mistakes discourage you. Learn from it and move forward. Understand what you want to achieve and why you want to achieve it. Decide what's important to you. Decipher between your wants and needs. You may have to let go of some of your wants right now. Disciplining yourself is key. Also, start saving early. Pay off debt (especially on things with high interest rates). Invest. Seek out a financial advisor to help you get familiar with different investment options and diversify your portfolio. Sign up for financial classes. I think it's also imperative to have multiple streams of income. Working a 9-5 job is great, and investments will provide another stream of income but also think about other things that you can do to supplement your income. (I love a good side hustle!) Last but not least, if you don't have a will or life insurance, get it NOW! Leave a legacy for your family, not a financial strain.

-What Can You Do Today To Increase Your Credit Score and Financial Status?-

Fading Friendships

I was once asked why do good friends grow apart after being close for many years. My response is that relationships change over time. And it's key to know when relationships NEED to change. Even the closest of friendships go through transition. People change, priorities change, situations change, and we are often forced to shift. Unfortunately, not everyone in your circle will be able or willing to shift accordingly. Not all of your friends will identify with the different stages in your life. And this often causes disunion. Don't feel bad or guilty about the transition. There is a season for everything. And sometimes certain relationships are good for only a season so just cherish the memories and always respect them for once being an intricate part of your life. Now on the other hand, there are some relationships built to last, and although the relationship shifts, it will still withstand the tests of time. Mature, authentic, lasting relationships take work though. You all must be very intentional about nurturing the friendship. None of us seem to have much time nowadays to get together one on one but it's important to try to invest some time for each other every now and then. The good thing about mature relationships is that even though things may start to look a little different, and time together may be limited, everyone is evolved enough to accept it and know that it's still solid. So as long as the friendship continues to uplift you and bring you some joy, and everyone is willing to be flexible in their expectations, you should treasure it and hold on to it. True friendships are a rare gift.

-Evaluate Your Friendships-

Gratitude

Some people will never realize what you bring to the table until you stop serving. Some people don't see all that you do, they only look at what you don't do. It's very easy for any of us to take things/people for granted which is why I'm a huge fan of keeping a gratitude journal. If you write down each day something that you're grateful for, it will remind you of the abundance in your life, who plays a part in that, and basically help you to focus on the good. It takes conscious effort to keep a thankful spirit. I think it's challenging for us humans because we have access to so much in life. Let's not take advantage of God's grace. Now when you feel that you're getting the short end of the stick and someone is taking you for granted, it may be necessary to express this to the person and see if a change can come about. Maybe they don't realize their ways. But in some situations it may be necessary to just no longer serve. Don't allow yourself to be used up by an ungrateful heart. You deserve to be appreciated and valued for what you do and who you are. Now in the same manner that someone is making you feel undervalued, please routinely check yourself and your relationships to ensure that you are not doing the same to others. Write in your gratitude journal, be a giver, stop expecting things, offer something back to someone that always goes out of their way to be there for you, and just take some time every now and then to simply say "I appreciate you." A little of that can go a long way.

-What Are You Grateful For Today?-

Purposed AND Polished

Mark Twain said "The two most important days in your life are the day you are born and the day you find out why." We all have a purpose to fulfill on this earth. Your spirit will not be at peace until you are walking effectively in your true, divine calling. It doesn't matter what you've done or what's currently going on in your life, your purpose awaits you and it will chase you down! Here are a few things to help you recognize and plan for it:

o What are your talents/ top skills? What are you really good at?

o Think about what you love to do.

o Consider what you value. What matters to you?

o Pray and seek direction and confirmation.

o Write down your vision – What do you want to achieve? What do you want to change? What do you want your life to look like tomorrow?

o Consider obstacles that might prevent you from birthing your vision. Expect and plan for them. Be confident that you can overcome them all.

o Write a personal mission statement. This will help you to discover more about yourself. List your goals, your core values, and your role. Review it often and live by it.

o Establish a detailed plan with timelines. Track your steps and celebrate each achievement.

o Ask God to bring someone into your life to mentor you, invest in you, and polish you.

o Go be great!

Polished Conversations

Nicole Ranée

authorHOUSE®

AuthorHouse™
1663 Liberty Drive
Bloomington, IN 47403
www.authorhouse.com
Phone: 1 (800) 839-8640

Published by AuthorHouse 06/14/2018

ISBN: 978-1-5462-4437-0 (sc)
ISBN: 978-1-5462-4435-6 (hc)
ISBN: 978-1-5462-4436-3 (e)

Library of Congress Control Number: 2018906526

Print information available on the last page.

King James Version (KJV)
Scriptures were taken from The King James Version of The Bible - Public Domain.

Contents

Everyone has a purpose. Knowing your purpose is an intricate part of life but walking effectively in your purpose is most essential. Many of us are not flowing in our purpose because we haven't been properly mentored and polished. We often neglect necessary self-reflection and refinement. We can't save others without first learning to save ourselves. Here is a collection of my outlook on a variety of topics that I think we sometimes miss but I believe will help you on your journey to becoming a powerful change agent in this world. Please take time to reflect and journal your thoughts, prayers, and ways to execute. I want to help encourage, sharpen and polish you. We all want to shine, right!?

Acknowledgments

I dedicate this book to my beautiful seeds, Xzavion and Sky. You two have always been my reason why. I love you more than words could ever express.

To my hubby, Sonny B. Thank you for pushing me, investing in me, and loving me back to life. You are my Superman. (And thanks for giving me super step children!)

Thanks to Nikki, Mario, and everyone that assisted me in any way on this book. I appreciate you immensely.

In loving memory of my mother Shirlene Carter, my father Wendell Carter, my brother James (Jim E.) Malcolm, and my grandmother Hattie Pearl Carter. You all are forever on my mind and in my heart.

Thank you to those that have poured into my life. Those that have spoken a word, led me to the Rock, and saw more in me than I saw in myself. I'm pressing toward the mark!

Mission: To Reach the Lost and Polish the Found

Who Are You?

Sometimes we can't get to where we need to be because we haven't dealt with where we are. During my workshops, I ask 'Who are you?' and we do ice breakers to get to know one another. I hear about children, careers, hobbies, etc. but after everyone has shared things about themselves, I then ask 'Who are you *really*?' I'm asking us to dig deeper. Too often we move routinely through our day to day life, saying we're okay when we're really not. It's time now to stop the façade and acknowledge who you are, and where you are. Allow yourself to feel what you feel. Honor yourself. Stand fearlessly in your authentic truth. We are all in different places at different times, and it's a different journey for everyone. Be gentle with yourself. God knows our struggles and wants to meet us right where we are. Psalm 103:14 says *'He knows our frame, and remembers that we are just dust.'* It's okay to not always be okay. We are 'just dust.' Acknowledgment is the first step to any healing, restoration and growth. Your healing will propel you into your purpose and will be a powerful contribution to the help and healing of others.

-What's In You That Needs Acknowledged?-

The Bent Woman

In Luke 13, the bible talks about a woman that was crippled by a spirit for 18 years. She was bent over, unable to straighten up. Studies show that people who suffer with back pain often find relief when they lean forward, thus with time, the spine often readjusts and before they know it they become permanently hunched over. What began with this woman's lower back pain, ended with a permanent deformity. What or who has bent you? And what are you willing to do to straighten up again? The scripture leads me to believe that at one time this woman walked straight and was able to look people in the eye but then somehow she was "crippled by a spirit". Something got ahold of her and altered her life. We don't know what happened but I do know that traumatic events in our lives can weaken and disfigure us. If you've spent 18 years of looking at the ground, you've missed out on a lot. Please don't get comfortable being in a hunched over state of mind. Don't allow some temporary relief from your pain to cause a permanent deformity in your life. Get to the root & to the Healer! *'He laid His hands on her; and immediately she was made straight, and glorified God!'* (See Luke 13:10-13)

-What Or Who Has Bent You?
What Are You Willing To Do
To Straighten Up Again?-

Guilt

Guilt and shame are two very toxic emotions. When you feel bad about yourself or what you've done, it will restrict you from producing. Guilt will keep you immobile. We've all done or said things that we regret. We've all made bad decisions. It's a part of this crazy thing called life and flesh. Yes, we have to deal with ourselves and our subsequent consequences but thank God for His grace and mercy! We just need to confess our wrong, and like Jesus told the woman caught in adultery (John 8:3-11) *'Go and sin no more.'* We'll never be perfect but sin must not be our lifestyle. Forgiveness should change us and move us into holiness. God's grace is sufficient and He uses damaged goods! He still loves you and has paid the ultimate price for you. He wants you to fulfill your purpose. You are enough! Don't allow others to make you feel inferior or diminish you. You are not who they criticized, marginalized, or scandalized you to be. You are EVERYTHING with God! A new creature. Redeemed! It's only the trick of the enemy to keep you bound by guilt and shame. Take off your grave clothes! Stop accessorizing the chains! Seek internal peace. I'm sure you've forgiven others from time to time so aren't you deserving of your own forgiveness? Receive it.

-What Guilt Do You Need To Release Today?-

Abracadabra

This word is synonymous with magic but what most don't know is that it's derived from an Aramaic phrase meaning "I create as I speak." Understand that your words are magical! Your words carry energy and impact. You can open up the atmosphere with your words! Affirm and command each day. Sometimes we dishonor who we are and hinder our objective just by the things we say. Recognize your power and speak the things that you desire. Call those things which be not as though they are! (see Rom 4:17) Pull from the spirit to the natural. The bible says *'Death and life are in the power of the tongue.'* (Prov 18:21) Speak positive, clean, edifying words. No more negative words. No more low-level conversations. There's nothing negative about God or His plan for our lives so protect your spirit, set the atmosphere, and speak LIFE!

-Shift The Atmosphere Right Now With Your Words-

Possession

During my time of jury duty, an attorney was describing the elements needed to indict for 'Possession'. She explained that a person can be charged with possessing something even if the object is not on them. There are two types of possession: Actual Possession and Constructive Possession. She gave an example of Constructive Possession using the pen in her pocket. She said "Even if I take this pen out of my pocket and put it on your desk, I still have power, dominion, and control over it. I plan to take it back." All I could think about then is how we all 'possess' something that God has given us or promised us. We may have put it on the shelf /desk for some time but we must remember that we still have dominion, power, and control over it! What have you put aside and forgotten about? I think it's time for you to go back and possess what's yours!

-What Do You Need To Reclaim?-

Control Your Emotions!

The funny thing about the brain is that it can't decipher what is real and what's not. This is why we cry at movies, or get emotionally worked up over just the thought of something that was said to us 10 years ago! When we think and feel something, we leave a mark in our brain so the more we think it and feel it, the deeper the impression gets. Mind your mind! Acknowledge and honor your feelings but don't stay stuck in emotions that do you no good. Don't let defeatist feelings gain momentum in your brain. Control your emotions, don't allow them to control you! Settle down, and make up your mind to do what's best and what's healthy for your spirit, regardless of the situation. Walk in obedience to God's word, and allow your emotions to catch up later!

-What Emotions Are Leading You?-

Perception

Per my doctor's suggestion, I had genetic counseling done assuming I'd be eligible for the genetic testing because cancer runs very high on my maternal side of the family as well as some on my paternal side. My mother died of cancer when I was only 27 years old. She was 58. To my surprise, I was not approved for the genetic testing because I am not considered high risk. This was great news but I must admit I was slightly surprised. I can name quite a few of my mother's siblings that died back to back of cancer. As a youngster, I was so tired of attending funerals and tired of hearing the word CANCER! Since then, I have feared that ugly word and have always thought our family was highly affected by it. That was my perception. Well, after sitting down with the counselor and drawing out our family tree, I realized that indeed there were a few that were affected by cancer but that few was out of a total of 17 children! That's not a high percentage (statistically speaking). So at that moment, my perception changed. My eyes were enlightened. Sometimes what we see or feel is not reflective of the whole picture, and not necessarily fact based. What I also didn't realize until this meeting was that most of the cancers that my family has had are not genetic cancers. They were lifestyle driven and/or random, not hereditary. This meeting turned out to be very enlightening, and pretty therapeutic. Something I had been carrying for 20 years regarding my mom's sickness (the 'maybe I should've'), I was finally able to release just from some medical information that Amie gave me that day. I cried like a baby! Again, my perception of the situation was not in full color detail. Unfortunately, our perception is our reality so I was living in that for years. This day was a great reminder that our viewpoint is not always accurate so it's best to not judge things on the surface. There are important details to every story, and things aren't always as they appear. Don't imprison yourself with

the 'what ifs'. Don't beat yourself up over things that you can't control now. We must try to make the best life decisions that we can but we never know God's plan so we must walk by faith and trust His hand. I believe the old gospel song is right "We'll understand it better by and by."

-In What Situation Might Your Perception Be Inaccurate?-

Don't Be Weary

One of my favorite scriptures is Galatians 6:9 *'And let us not be weary in well doing, for in due season, we shall reap if we faint not.'* Life happens, and it's very hard sometimes to stay encouraged and on your square. Satan's goal is to wear you down and make you abort your path to purpose. Don't give in. And don't stand still. Standing still in your spiritual life is like standing still in the midst of a gushing river. You are either moving upstream or being pushed downstream. When you doubt how far you can go, just look at how far you've already come. Stay encouraged and push through in faith. My testimony is like David's *'I would've fainted had I not believed to see the goodness of the Lord in the land of the living!'* (PS 27:13) Please don't get weary. You may not see the situation changing in the manner that you'd like or as soon as you'd like, and you may not receive a pat on the back like you deserve but keep doing well. The Lord sees you, hears you, and will perfect that which concerneth you. (See PS 138:8)

-Write A Mantra Of Encouragement For Yourself-

I'm Only Human

This is a common phrase but let's admit it's a common cop out as well. People talk about how human they are but let's talk about how holy you are! We are the righteousness of God (see 2 Cor 5:21), and Romans 8:17 reminds us that we are joint heirs with Christ so if we share in His sufferings, we'll also share in His glory! Yes, we're only human but God has given us all things pertaining to life and godliness, and through His promises we can be partakers of His divine nature. The more you grow in knowledge of the scriptures, the more your heart will be convicted and your path made right. You'll also discover your power through Him. He is our strength in weakness. Where we stop is where He begins. If we're in connection and right relationship with Him then we should bear good fruit. No more excuses. We must stop focusing on our humanity, and start walking more in our divinity!

-In What Areas Do You Need To Stop Making Excuses?-

Myopia

I've worn glasses since middle school. I have poor distance vision. The medical term for my condition is Myopia or Myopic vision. It is commonly known as nearsightedness or short sight. I can see up close but need corrective lenses to see things far away. My eye condition is not fatal but I've learned that having a Myopic view in life can be! If you are narrow-minded, lack in imagination, and can't see past your current situation, you have a similar Myopic view! You are greater than who you presently are. You are more than what you've become. Look past your nose, catch a vision for your life, and pursue it! Proverbs 29:18 says *'Where there is no vision, the people perish.'* Without vision, we are in darkness. Always look ahead and aim high. Having a clear vision will lead you and guide you in setting goals, making plans, making decisions, and evaluating your work. A clear vision will keep you forward focused and will help you fulfill your purpose. Like an architect, envision your next new beautiful life building, and know that you are the master designer!

-Cut And Paste Images From Magazines Onto A Poster Board And Create Your Vision Board.-

Derailed by Distractions

When I was a youngster doing my dreaded homework, my mind would often drift and I'd start thinking about what I was going to wear to school the next day. Sometimes I'd have music playing and when my favorite part of the song came on, of course I had to stop and sing every word! Most of the time I'd have the TV on and that was a huge distraction. It doesn't matter if we enjoy the task at hand or not, becoming distracted seems inevitable. I think distractions now are worse than they were when I was a kid because we now have digital distractions. It took me longer to write this book than it probably should have because instead of being focused, I was distracted by emails, text messages, Facebook, Snapchat, Twitter, you name it! Distractions are a sure way of keeping us from producing. Relationships are affected by distractions. Workplace production is low due to distractions. And sadly, people are injured and killed because of distracted drivers. Technology is wonderful but we must be mindful of how much distraction they cause in our lives. Maybe it's a person or relationship that's a distraction for you. Distractions will hinder productivity, snuff out creativity, and move you away from your purpose. Don't let that happen. Clear your mind, plan your day, eliminate distractions as much as possible (i.e. turn off your phone), and remember the value of the work that you're doing. People think they need more hours in the day when really they just need more motivation and determination. Stay on course. You've got dreams to keep and goals to meet. Focus, function, and finish.

-What Has Your Attention?-

Leadership

Many people want to lead but have never been good at following. Many desire a position and title but they lack a heart to serve. We should all strive to be a servant leader like Jesus. My position may be above you but my attitude and heart should be among you. An effective leader is not caught up on titles, and they're willing to put in the work for the greater good. A servant leader is not above assisting you on a project, even bringing you coffee, or listening and encouraging you with life issues. There's an open door policy and that leader seeks diverse opinions. A good leader encourages & develops others and is not threatened by their potential and growth. Before you seek leadership, please make sure you have a heart for the people and a desire to disciple them and help them grow and go. You should not be upset when they are ready to branch out into deeper waters. You should groom them with that being the ultimate goal. In John 14, Jesus told his disciples that He has shown them the way so they should be able to do greater works than even He did. Leaders should want to create, mold and polish others to be leaders! If you desire leadership, sit under a good leader. Learn and develop. Don't worry about being overlooked and try to force your way into a leadership position. The bible says *'A man's gift will make room for him and bring him before great men.'* (Prov 18:16) Work in your gifting, sharpen your skills, and ask God to prepare your heart to be a servant leader.

-What More Can You Do To Display Your Servant-Leader Heart?-

Everything you want, BE.

We attract who we are. Too often we expect others to be something that we aren't reflecting. Don't expect others to do what you're not doing. Raise your own bar and then you can raise the standard of what you will allow. You teach people how to treat you. They will only go as far as you will let them. Attract the positives of what you want by setting the boundaries. For example, if you want that man to hold the door for you, don't walk in until he does! Train your thoughts, be intentional in your actions, and conscious of your display. Surround yourself with people that are where you want to be. Do whatever you need to do to be who you want so that you'll get what you desire!

-What Am I Attracting? Is It What I Want?-

Inquire

Who do they say that you are? Sometimes it's good to inquire and listen to what others say about you… even if it's not so pleasing. If you find yourself constantly the common denominator in chaos and drama, there may be some truth about yourself that you need to recognize. Do you often offend people? Is your name always in the middle of mess? If you have issues with numerous people, YOU are the common denominator and maybe you're a sower of discord that the bible talks about in Proverbs 6. I know it's hard to look in the mirror at the flaws but constant growth should be your ultimate goal. Ask God to show you your ways. Another aspect to inquiring is that maybe people speak highly of you in a certain area. Sometimes we need to just hear and receive that. I didn't realize in myself that I was an effective communicator and exhorter until people actually spoke it into my life, and I finally listened.

-Are You The Common Denominator In Chaos And Drama? If So, Why?-

Complacency Kills!

—⌇—

I love myself! I really do. However, I am fully cognizant of the fact that I have not yet "arrived" in any area of my life, and frankly, I don't ever want to feel like I've "arrived". Even in my forties, I yearn to learn, grow, and produce! Unfortunately, there are times in which I get into a slump and I become complacent. Well, I know I can't get stuck there because COMPLACENCY KILLS! Whether in the workplace, professional life, or personal life, complacency will lead to downfall. The definition of complacency is 1. Smug satisfaction with one's self or one's achievements. 2. Being overly satisfied or comfortable with an existing situation or condition, often while unaware of potential dangers or deficiencies… Dangers or Deficiencies! Please think about that for a moment. Sadly, we're often not even aware of how deficient we are! It's imperative that we get out of our comfort zones, accept challenges, and push ourselves to evolve daily. Love yourself, celebrate your successes but don't ever get fully satisfied with where you are and what you are. Don't get stuck. Evolve daily!

-In What Area Should You Be Producing More?-

Stay Hungry

Most animals will hunt, catch, and devour a good meal. After they've eaten, they get full and content. But this state of contentment and satisfaction then makes them the easy prey. Do you remember when you were hungry and determined!? What is it in your life now that has you feeling full? What is causing you to be content and no longer want to chase your dreams? Have you reached your destiny or are you just comfortable? Don't sit stagnant and become easy prey for the enemy (AKA the dream killer). Pay attention to spiritual things. Your soul has a way of letting you know when you're spiritually hungry. I remember a time when I was irritable and restless but didn't understand why. Things on the surface were going well in my life yet I felt discontented. Well, my spirit was growling from hunger! We can try to fill ourselves with all other things pertaining to success and happiness but we'll always feel a certain void if we neglect feeding our spirit with the presence of God and His word. It all works together. Feed your spirit and stay chasing!

-What Is Your Spirit Growling For?-

Grief

The grieving process is different for everyone, and there's no time limit nor is there an instruction manual on how to grieve. We all must go through our own process. I just want you to know that God collects all of your tears (see PS 56:8), even the ones you've held back or cried silently. He knows what you're going through and He cares. After the death of my mother (my best friend), and then my father, there were days I felt so alone and it took every fiber of my being to even get out of the bed. Thankfully, before my beautiful parents left this earth, they gave me the gift of a spiritual foundation so I was able to mourn with some faith in God's goodness and wisdom. The bible tells us that as Christians we are not to grieve like those without hope. (1Thes 4:13-14) *'Weeping may endure for a night but joy comes in the morning.'* (PS 30:5). You will smile, laugh, and be happy again, and yes, that's okay. Being happy does not dishonor your loved one. Give yourself permission to laugh through the tears. There's healing in it. *'And after you have suffered for a little while, the God of all grace will perfect, establish, strengthen and settle you.'* (see 1 Peter 5:10)

-Have You Allowed Yourself To Grieve? Have You Allowed Yourself To Smile Through Your Tears?-

Quasi-Relationships

We all desire companionship and to feel loved. Some of us desire it so much that whenever we get a little attention from someone we want to call it "love" because we don't know what other box to put it in. If we're honest though, we know that it's not a good, healthy relationship of love. We've settled for a quasi-relationship with the appearance of being real but not quite. Next thing you know you lose focus of yourself, your purpose and goals. You invest time and energy into a quasi-relationship which often turns toxic and gets you off your square, and then you can't seem to shake it because you're gripped by the strongholds of this unhealthy soul tie. Be careful of the trick of the enemy. The bible says we are not ignorant of the devil's devices. (See 2 Cor 2:11) Lust of the flesh and sexual sin will take you further than you want to go. I was a pretty good girl growing up. I came from a two-parent household in which both parents were wonderful, hardworking, and church going but sexual sin was my demon. I married my high school sweetheart who later turned preacher/pastor so I was a Pastor's wife (aka "First Lady") for a short time until sexual sin (adultery) overtook him and we ended up divorced after 16 years. Well, after our divorce I was a mess, looking for love in all the wrong places. Settling, losing pieces of myself bit by bit. I was confused. Couldn't comprehend why God had poured so much into me only to end up a divorced preacher's wife and mother of two. I definitely couldn't see past where I was at that moment. Some time later, I decided to visit my cousin Marlo's church and this pastor whom I'd never met before, preached about unhealthy soul ties. I swear he was talking directly to me! Then after the sermon he called me out to come up for prayer. That man prayed and prophesied as if Jesus Himself was speaking directly in his ear about my life. He told me I must free myself of the soul tie. He said that I was in such a state of confusion that I couldn't make a good decision even if I tried.

Thankfully he went on to say that God wanted to restore me and restore everything that I had lost and that I'd rise up like Esther! It took me a minute to release myself of quasi-relationships and self sabotage but one day I finally did. I truly surrendered, trusted God and found a state of contentment. Months passed and I was feeling good and content with my alone time, yet somehow still confident that God would send real love my way. I didn't know how or with who but I believed it and before long He indeed did just that. My now husband pursued me properly. Left no question in my mind of his effort, his intent, and his long-term purpose. He did everything that Steve Harvey says a man will do if he's genuine and plans to make you his wife – Pursue, Provide, Profess, and Protect. No games. Stop settling for something that just resembles what you're looking for. Remember your worth. Stop investing in quasi-relationships, and getting no good return on your investment. You're better than that, and God is bigger than that!

-Is There An Unhealthy Soul Tie That You Need To Cut?-

Transparency

Visible. Free from pretense or deceit. I wish more of us would be transparent in our dealings and relationships. Too often, we want people to think we are more than what we are, or we feel differently than what we portray. You can't seek counseling and say you want restoration if you're not willing to be transparent. We want to tell our version of the story and make people side with us but in all honesty we haven't fully disclosed the not-so-pretty details that may reflect our flaws or mistakes in the situation. I was in my car one night listening to a radio talk show with a financial expert on as a guest, and a woman called in for advice. She briefly explained her situation and asked him if he thought it was a good idea. The advisor started asking her questions in which she gave answers to but I sensed that she was omitting some important details. Please don't ask someone for their help and advice if you're not going to be forthright. It dishonors the whole process. We must be authentic if we want to progress. Maybe the reason we're not able to be transparent with others is because we're in denial and not even transparent with ourselves! When the children of Israel were in the wilderness (see Exodus 16), they were so tired and frustrated. They didn't understand what God was doing so they complained and basically said 'Man we had it better back in Egypt! At least we had plenty of good food to eat!' Sure, transition can be uncomfortable but transparency is a must. They wanted to go back to the 'good ol days' but if they were being honest, they would've admitted that it wasn't all that great for them back in the day because there they were still slaves! I realized in my personal life that I did the same thing. I sometimes considered going backwards because I thought it was better than the uncomfortable moment that I was in but I wasn't being fully transparent about the past. My 'Egypt' was where I experienced heart break, a confidence shake, embarrassment, and pain. Be real and deal. And don't forget to be transparent with yourself.

-Have You Been Honest With Yourself?-

Destination Addiction

Too often we create a picture in our mind of what our life should look like (what, when, and with who), and we allow others to influence our thoughts of what our life should be. Too often we're stressed and frustrated because we planned something different than what we currently have. We often try to have it all figured out and we end up pushing against what God has for us because it's not how we envisioned it so we keep searching for more, jumping from one thing to the next. An unknown author once said "Beware of Destination Addiction – a preoccupation with the idea that happiness is in the next place, the next job, with the next partner. Until you give up the idea that happiness is somewhere else, it will never be where you are." I love this quote because many of us are constantly searching for the 'next big thing' but overlook or under appreciate the present blessings in our lives. It's great to want more but don't miss or minimize what you have in this moment because you're worried about the next. Life is ever changing. The bible tells us to be faithful over small things so that we can be entrusted with more. (see Matt 25:23) It's not just about reaching your destination, it's important to be fully present and grateful in the moment right where you are.

-Where Do You Need To Be More Present?-

Unforgiveness

You cannot fully walk in your purpose if you're bearing bitterness and unforgiveness in your heart. The enemy's most powerful strategy against us is unforgiveness. God will not hear our prayers if we harbor the sin of unforgiveness. God will not forgive us our sins if we will not forgive others. (review Matt 6:1-4) Satan wants to keep us outside of God's will, and unforgiveness is a great way to do just that. Isn't it more important to get what God has for you than to hold on to what others have done to you!? Yes, forgiveness is not easy (and doesn't always seem fair) but it's necessary. Even if the other person doesn't seek reconciliation, you must take the high road and do what's needed to free your own soul from anger and bitterness. Some relationships are worth redeeming, while others you may have to simply release and let go. If you care enough to try to redeem, please remember to focus on the value of the person, not the behavior. If you say you forgive, then truly forgive. Don't use the past as a weapon when it's convenient. Wipe the slate clean. When God forgives us, He remembers our sin no more. (see Heb 8:12) Don't try to use all the grace for yourself and not extend any to others.

-Who Do You Need To Forgive?-

Don't Miss Your Moment

Jesus probably would have kept walking and passed up blind Bartimaeus had he not yelled out 'Son of David, have mercy on me!' Jesus probably would not have stopped had Jairus not caught His attention and pleaded for him to see about his sick daughter! Would Jesus have healed the woman with the issue of blood had she not fought through the crowd to touch the hem of his garment!?? I don't want to ever come that close to Jesus and MISS Him! God is always on the move. It's on us to keep moving, cry out, get through the crowd, and get His attention! Don't be so consumed with yourself and your issues that you miss your day of visitation!

-What Are You Willing To Do To Get Jesus' Attention?-

Grab and Hold

In life, some of us TOUCH a whole lot of things but never really HOLD them. Why is that? Do we fear commitment? Is it fear of failure? Fear of the unknown? Lack of control? Pride? Lack of confidence? What stands between you and a chance at happiness and success? What keeps you from walking in your purpose? Don't lose out on life's gifts and opportunities by allowing fear to paralyze you! Face it, embrace it, push through it. Eleanor Roosevelt said "Do it afraid." Sure, there's no guarantee in life (or love) but a part of living is taking chances and allowing yourself to be vulnerable. With that, you may just stumble upon your greatest gift of all. Step out of the zone of your comfort. Don't just touch... Sometimes it's worth it to grab & HOLD!

-What Stands Between You And A Chance At Happiness And Success?-

An Indolent Mentality

Merriam-Webster's definition of Indolent: 'Averse to activity, effort, or movement. Showing an inclination to laziness. Slow to develop or heal. Causing little or no pain.' I don't think any one of us want to admit that we're lazy but I'm sure that there are areas in which we can all better ourselves and push out a little more. For me, procrastination has always been my downfall. I tend to want to put off something until tomorrow when I could feasibly do it today. Sometimes we're not where we want to be simply because we're not putting in the work. The other part of the definition of indolent is slow to develop or heal. Are you not progressing in your life because you haven't healed? Are you not taking the steps to develop? Take action. Someone somewhere is waiting for you to produce.

-What's Your Downfall That's Keeping You From Progressing?-

T.E.A. *Time*

I love tea. There are many types of tea with numerous health benefits. Green Tea and Black Tea have been found to be great for heart health. White Tea is a great antioxidant. Oolong Tea is popular for weight loss, and my favorite is Chai Tea. There's pretty much a tea for everyone! And honestly, I think I love tea parties as much as I love tea! I love dressing up, and I love the intimate fellowship with other women. Years ago, I used to work with my cousin, and whenever I sensed that she was a little disturbed by something, I would ask if she wanted to have "Tea Time" in her office. At first, she thought I was crazy & told me she didn't like tea. Then she understood and it became a 'thing' with us. On her rough days she would say "Girl, we need to have tea!" Although we never consumed any beverage in her office, our connection, encouragement, & conversations were incredible. I'm not exactly sure why I started using that term but I ran with it & I'm a believer that we all need a little T.E.A. Time which I identify as **T**ransparent **E**dification & **A**ccountability. Find a friend that will build you up, hold you up, as well as hold you accountable, and make sure you get together often for T.E.A.

-When's Your Tea Party And Who's Invited?-

Delivered

As I write this book, I'm inspired by our beloved "Mother" Mary Beets who is a beautiful woman who will love you to pieces with her welcoming spirit, she will preach and teach you the Word of God, and she will come up with theee best sayings! One of my favorite Mary Beets' quotes is "Get delivered from people!" Stop wasting time worrying about what others think about you. You don't need people to sign off on what God has purposed in you. Do what you're called to do, whether people like it, support it, or not. People have no hell to put you in nor a heaven to keep you out of. I've learned that people usually do things, think things, and say things birthed from their own experiences, motives, and sometimes insecurities. Often how people feel about us is not really about us. Pray for them. Like I mentioned, Mother Beets is a very sweet, loving person so please make sure you too exemplify love and grace, walk upright, treat people according to God's Word but don't get hung up on seeking the approval of others. I know in this day and age, we all tend to want "Friends" and "Followers" but we don't need people to just "Like" what we do. Ask God to give you an inner circle of people to love, support, and push you. In the meantime, remember my favorite quote by Zig Ziglar: "You had a purpose before anyone had an opinion."

-Why Are You Allowing The Opinion Of Others To Affect You?-

Word

It's so hard for me to listen to someone giving a presentation, speech, or sermon, and the content is good but the delivery is grueling. It's torture sometimes to sit through, and most people won't stay engaged at all. Words are important and your delivery of them can be a game changer. Have you ever been accused of coming off harshly with your words but you didn't intend it to be that way? Well, the old adage is true – It's not what you say but how you say it. Delivery is everything. I've never been a loud, confrontational person so I wasn't aware that the mere inflection of my voice caused my words to sometimes sound abrasive. I was quite surprised when I was informed of this but rather than saying "that's just the way I am", I started to make a conscious effort to really think about what I want to say and to be careful in how I say it, especially when having crucial conversations. Words are forever, and I want to edify with my words. Sometimes we have to undo the way we've always been. I strive to be a strong woman with a soft heart, and I want my words to line up with that. We don't have to be sharp with our words to get our point across. People are typically more receptive to respectful, polished conversations. Ghandi once said "In a gentle way you can shake the world."

-What Can You Do To Enhance Your Delivery?-

A Giver

The great orator Maya Angelou once said "Giving liberates the soul of the giver." I wish we would recognize that more and take pride in giving and serving. *'For God so loved the world, that He gave His only begotten Son.'* (John 3:16) We are saved because God *gave* His son Jesus who *gave* up His life to save ours. We are called to be Christ like so why is it so hard for some of us to be cheerful givers? Jesus said *'It is more blessed to give than to receive.'* (Acts 20:35) Some of us hold on so tight to what we have as if we don't understand that God gave it and can take it away from us at any given moment. Everything we have is from Him – our money, our talent, our time. Many people attend church regularly but are reluctant to give their tithes and offerings because they're afraid of what the money will be used for. We are commanded to give, and in most cases, your gift will be appreciated but nowhere in the bible does it say anything about giving only if you're acknowledged, appreciated, and know exactly what happens next with your gift. If you offer shoes to someone and they decide later to sell them, so what!? If someone from the church unethically uses the money that you gave in tithes then the blood will be on their hands, not yours. God will deal with them, and you'll still be blessed! In Malachi 3:10 the Lord tells us to bring our tithes and offerings, and then tells us to test Him. *'Test me in this, says the Lord, and see if I won't open the floodgates of heaven and pour you out a blessing that you won't have room enough to receive!'* Please make sure you understand this entire scripture. He'll bless our socks off if we do what he commands us to do. The more we give, the more we will get in return, and others will see our obedience and faith, and glorify God.

-How Will You Increase Your Giving?-

Fight!

The bible says that Satan should not get an advantage of us because we are not ignorant of his devices. (see 2 Cor 2:11) So why do you act so surprised when the attacks come your way? Things can be going well and then suddenly you're hit with a situation that almost knocks you off your feet. Don't let it. Satan is on his job. We just need to be on ours! Recognize that it's spiritual warfare. Stand up and fight in the spirit! Our plans, our responsibilities, our vision, our mission, our purpose will be tested. The closer you get to becoming all that God created you to be, the more warfare will increase in your life. You are on the brink of a breakthrough. Cry out for extraordinary grace! No matter the situation, seek God, trust God, and also ask Him to show you yourself during this time. There's a lesson in every test that God allows into our lives. We are not exempt from trials and tribulations but they are intended to stretch us and make us stronger, not kill us. Don't give up, don't give in, and don't stagger at the promises of God through unbelief. Employ desperate faith! Face your fears, and no matter the circumstance, remind yourself that God is still good!

-What Current Situation Do You Recognize As Spiritual Warfare? Fight In The Spirit!-

Effective Communication

We all desire to be understood. Good communication is how we articulate and convey what we think and feel. We cannot expect people to know what we want or need without communicating it. Communication rids assumptions and misunderstandings. Speak up – even if your voice shakes. My parents used to say "A closed mouth won't get fed." And if you're unsure about something or you've been hurt by what someone has said or done, communicate it. With that being said, don't forget that listening is an imperative part of communication too. There's nothing more frustrating than speaking to someone who is clearly not engaged and listening to you. We must know how to listen and receive. Don't listen with an urgency to respond, listen with an intent to understand. Effective communication will help us in building relationships and in resolving differences.

-What Steps Do You Need To Take To Ensure Better Communication?-

Intentional

It's always good to have a plan. We often focus on our long-term goals but neglect to be intentional in our daily journey. Sometimes our goals appear lofty and can become overwhelming, so I think the key is to focus on small steps that will get you to your ultimate goal. And don't forget to celebrate those small achievements. It's important to be intentional in our daily plan because we are all just one bad choice away from success, one toxic relationship away from disaster. Keep your eye on the prize! Have a plan, be deliberate, be intentional! I also want to encourage you to be intentional every day with self care. Commit time for YOU. Also, intentionally think about small things that you can do to bring joy to someone else. Suggestions: Give at least 3 compliments daily. Volunteer/ Donate. Attend a community event. Pray with someone. Give blood. Pay for someone's meal. Tell someone they matter.

-What Will You Intentionally Do This Week?-

Commitment Under Fire

A young man told me the other day that he felt like going back to the streets because he doesn't feel like he's getting ahead by doing things the right way. It's easy to get discouraged when you're trying to do the right things in life yet obstacles, roadblocks, and delays seem to consistently come your way. I just want to remind you that we've all experienced this to varying degrees but these are temporary situations only to force you into deeper levels of commitment. Please don't let the fire consume you! Keep committed to the commitment that you made to yourself (not to mention others). Don't change positions, just grow and develop right in the place that you're in! These moments are meant to be teachable moments for us – maybe teaching patience, prayer, perseverance, faith... When you can't see the end of the stormy road just believe that it's there. Storms don't last forever. Then when you're strengthened, please don't forget to turn around & strengthen someone else. Life is a journey, and someone out there is watching how you travel. Stay strong, stay encouraged, stay committed.

-Write Down The Names Of A Few People That Might Be Watching How You Travel. Let That Motivate You.-

Indecision

Indecision is usually caused by fear. Of course take time to think and pray things through but there comes a point in which you must trust your gut, your heart, God's leading, and walk confidently in a decision. Please know that indecision is a decision and affects everything. I had a friend that was separated from her (now) ex-husband but there was a time in which they talked of possible reconciliation. He led her to believe that he was considering moving back closer so that they could maybe "date" again. Time passed, emotions mixed, more time passed and nothing happened. His indecision was a decision and she finally had to realize and release that. Don't be indecisive and don't let others lead you on their path of cowardly indecisiveness. Teddy Roosevelt once said "The best thing you can do is the right thing. The next best thing is the wrong thing. The worst thing is nothing." Failure to decide is sure failure to succeed – in relationships, business, anything! Check yourself. Somewhere deep inside you know what it is, you know what you want and need. Just take the steps to do it.

-Where Is Indecision Playing
A Role In Your Life?-

The Fixer Upper

My children will tell you, and my husband can attest to the fact that I am a fixer. If they tell me they're in a situation, my brain will immediately start working overtime to figure out how I can assist. I always thought this was a good trait, however, when my husband had a small crisis, I was giving suggestions and offering to do things to help resolve the situation, and to my surprise, he told me to stop and let him handle it. He went on to say that I don't need to fix everything. I was taken aback, and honestly my feelings were hurt a little because my intentions were pure. I was just trying to help and be a good wife. Well, he is a grown man and guess what? He worked it out and didn't need my assistance. Now please believe, we're still a team, as husband and wife should be, and we're there to lift each other up but I've learned that not all battles are for me to fight. And as my children have turned into adults, I have really realized that I don't need to try to fix everything, nor *can* I fix everything. Sometimes we have to let our loved ones experience life and learn to problem solve for themselves. I love my children but when challenges arise, I don't want them to immediately depend on me. I want them to depend on God and seek His direction. There are teachable moments in our predicaments, and I don't want to hinder anyone's growth. Now I'd be remiss if I didn't take a moment to urge you ladies to stop trying to fix these men that you're dating! Like houses, some are older and run down yet still valuable and full of character so it may be worth investing in and fixing up. While others, are just too far gone and it would take too much out of you to dump money and time into it. Being a nurturer is an honorable thing but you can't save the world, and some things aren't meant to be fixed. Even in counseling, you have to counsel with detachment. You can offer your best but people must ultimately choose what they want in their lives. They

have to want to be "fixed" and willing to go through the process. It's disheartening if they choose otherwise but you can't be attached to the outcome. Do what you're called to do but rid yourself of the pressure to fix everything and everybody.

-What Can You Fix? What Should You Forget?-

Confident, yet Humble

I think a lot of Christians need polished in this area. I've met many people that walk in confidence, knowing who they are in Christ, and quoting scriptures to confirm, constantly saying 'Lord, Lord' yet they come off arrogant to others. Yes, you are a royal priesthood, you are a chosen people (see 1 Peter 2:9), you are fearfully and wonderfully made (PS 139:14), you are the head and not the tail (see Deu 28:13) but being arrogant and puffed up is not of God. There's an old saying "Don't be so heavenly minded that you're no earthly good." We should all be certain and bold, yet flow with humility. Throughout my life, I've been complimented on many different things but what I most cherish is when someone speaks of my sweet spirit. That just warms my soul. I first remember hearing the Beatitudes from my grandmother Hattie P. Carter who had the sweetest spirit ever, and two of the Beatitudes that I remember her quoting most are *'Blessed are the pure in heart for they shall see God.'* (Matt 5:8) and *'Blessed are the meek for they shall inherit the earth.'* (Matt 5:5). Walking meekly and humbly with a pure spirit yet confidently and boldly can be a challenge. We have to die to our flesh daily to achieve it but it is an absolute must! Don't blow your testimony and chance to be a light for someone by coming off arrogant, judgmental, and vainglorious. Be confident yet loving, be confident yet humble, be confident yet merciful. In other words, be like Christ.

-Is Your Light Shining Brightly
Or Is It Being Dimmed
By Your Arrogance?

The Submitted Wife

Submission is not a bad word. We all submit daily to either God or the devil. We submit to something or someone all the time. We submit to traffic lights and laws of the land. We submit to our employers and company policies. And although the bible specifically tells wives to submit to their husbands (Eph 5:22), we seem to struggle with this one. Maybe it's because we don't finish the rest of the scripture. It says '*Wives, submit yourselves unto your husband, as unto the Lord.*' When you stop looking at him (the man) and do it as unto the Lord, your perspective and motivation should shift. I know it's much easier to submit to a man that's submitted to God so prayerfully you have chosen a man seeking to do God's will; However, 1 Peter 3:1 says '*Wives, in the same way, submit yourselves to your husbands, so that if they obey NOT the word, they may without the word be won by the conversations/behaviors of the wives.*' Now let that marinate. And don't worry ladies, God has specific instructions for the husbands too, just do what you're commanded to do… as unto the Lord.

-How Can You Be A More Submissive Wife?-

Remember

I love journaling, and highly suggest everyone do it regularly. My memory is not the greatest so looking back occasionally through my journal helps remind me of beautiful, joyful moments. It also gives me my faith references. I find LIFE when I read about dismal situations that only God could turn in my favor and He did just that! When I start to get discouraged, I have references to remind me that if He did it before, He can do it again! Hebrews 11 talks about faith references. Abraham was tested to offer his son Isaac as a sacrifice and told to go to an unknown place and by faith he received the blessings of the promised land. Sarah thought she was too old to conceive, Noah was warned about things not seen, and God showed himself strong and faithful in their situations! What powerful faith references for them. I can look back after my divorce and know that is was through God's grace that I was able to live on my own and raise two children while making only $12/hour with no child support. God didn't forget about little ol' me. By faith, we lacked nothing! What's your faith reference? Surely God has blessed you and come through on your behalf in many ways so you should think on those things during your dark moments and faith your way through. It's time to live this thing out!

-What Are Some Of Your Faith References?-

Good Medicine

Anyone that knows me well, knows that I love to laugh… a lot! I've been told that my smile is bright and my laugh is contagious, and I hope it is because I'm a firm believer that laughter is good for the soul. Proverbs 17:22 says *'A merry heart does good like a medicine; But a broken spirit dries the bone.'* I don't have time for dryness! I take my laughter RX daily! Regardless of day-to-day circumstances, we must find joy in this journey. Joy can suffocate pain. Most things that you're stressing about right now, are things that will end up being minimal in the grand scheme of things. A year from now you'll look back and wonder why you allowed it to steal your joy. Get up, dress up, lighten up, and laugh! We all face challenges but how we respond to them is what's important. Keep pushing, praying, and keep smiling!

-Have You Laughed Today?-

NO!

Offering help to others is usually an honorable thing but being a people pleaser can be self-detrimental. If you constantly do things for others because you're concerned about what they will think or say, then you're doing it for the wrong reasons, and could ultimately be to your detriment. It's ok to sometimes say no. It's ok to change your mind. It's ok to not attend and help with every event. It's ok to not answer that call. It's ok to disagree and do something different than what others think you should do. Don't feel guilty about it. Let your no be no! Don't spread yourself so thin that you can't enjoy your own life and meet your own desires. Devoting so much to everyone else probably means you're leaving very little for yourself.

-What Do You Need To Say No To Today?-

It Won't Stop Hurting

I remember watching a criminal tv series one night, and the investigators were on the hunt to find a serial kidnapper. Well, when they captured the kidnapper, they realized it was a young woman that had been a victim of a serious crime herself and had lost her son. As they handcuffed her, she screamed and cried "It won't stop hurting!" Those words penetrated my heart and resonated with me. It's true, hurt people hurt people. Is there a significant wound in your life that has not healed? Unhealed wounds have a way of creeping up on us and manifesting in unhealthy ways. You cannot stay in a place of hurt without hurting yourself and/ or others. Confess and unpack the pain. Seek restoration and healing for that sore spot. Go to counseling. Do the work. You can get through it. You may have scars to show but you can surely heal.

-What Pain Do You Need To Unpack?-

Discipline and Accountability

Disciplining yourself is never easy but worth it. Discipline is what it takes to make things become habit and a way of life. Because it's often difficult to consistently do the things that we are called to do (whether it's to exercise or be a godly spouse, etc.) it's important to have an accountability partner. We all need someone to encourage and support us, as well as confront us, tell us about ourselves, and sharpen us. *'Iron sharpens iron, so a man sharpeneth the countenance of his friend.'* (Prov 27:17) Find a good accountability partner and be a good accountability partner for someone. None of us are above the other but we can still pour into each other and hold each other accountable. We're in this thing together.

-In What Area Do You Need To Be More Disciplined? Who Is Your Accountability Partner?-

How Do You Leave People?

How do people feel, what do people say after an encounter with you? Uplifted, empowered, happy, hopeful? Or down, drained, exhausted, discouraged? Energy is transferrable. Attitudes are contagious. Is yours worth catching? You may be the best of the best in your field but your character will outweigh your accomplishments. How you make people feel is more impactful that any service they may receive from you. Be careful to not burn bridges after ending professional or personal relationships. How you leave one thing is usually how you begin the next.

-How Do You Leave People?-

Printed in the United States
By Bookmasters